This Book Belongs To

WILD NATURE

ADULT COLORING BOOK
24 STRESS RELIEVING DESIGNS

Enjoy this wonderful collection of 24 Wild Nature designs that you will love coloring. Escape to a world of creative inspiration and joy. Lions, Elephants, Whales and Wolves await you at every turn of the page. We hope that our intricate line drawings will help generate quietness and wellness in your mind as you watch your creations come to life. Printed on one side only.

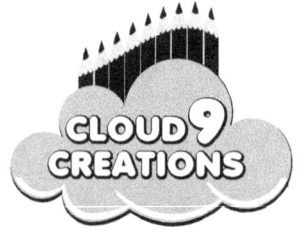

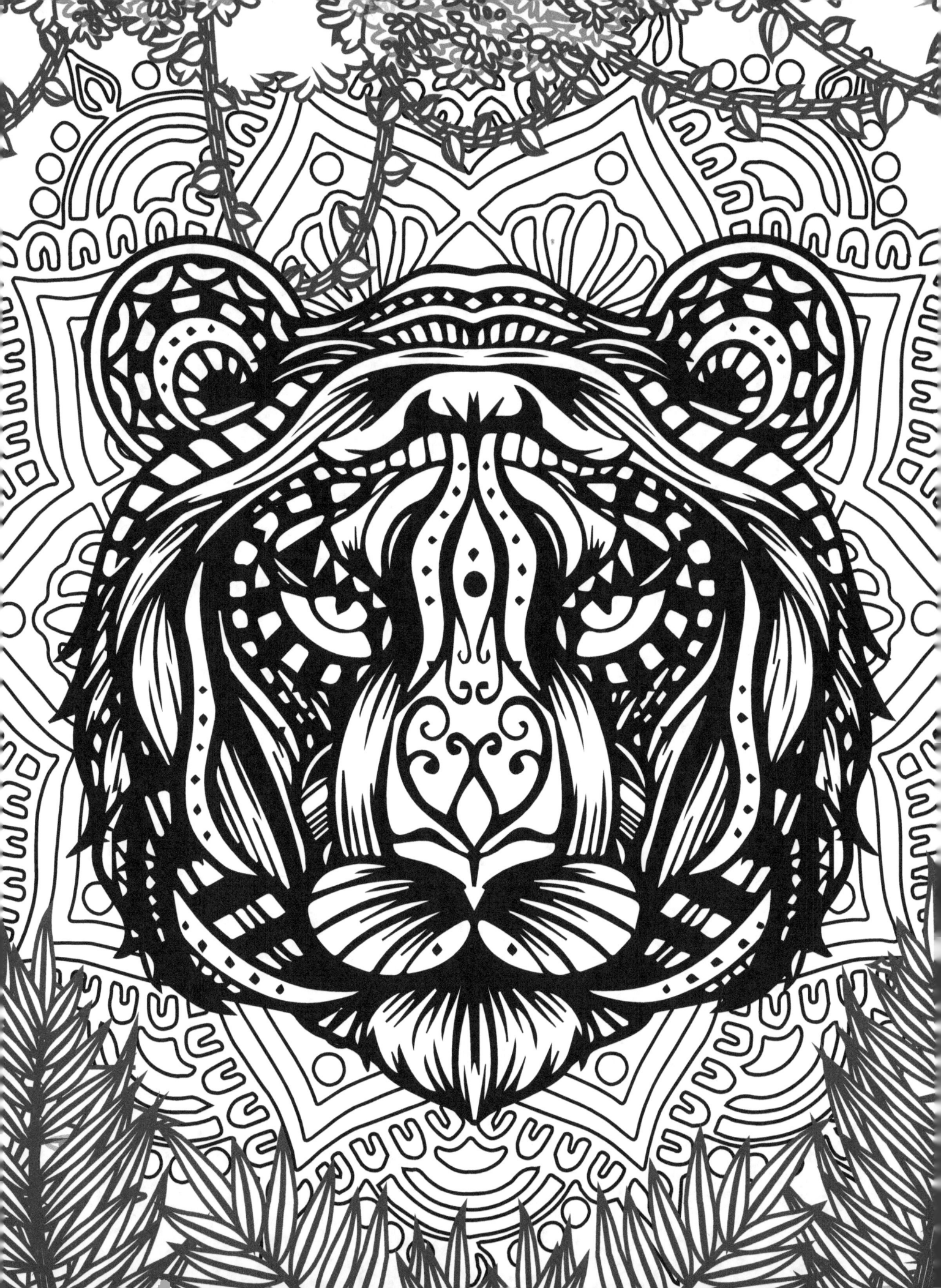

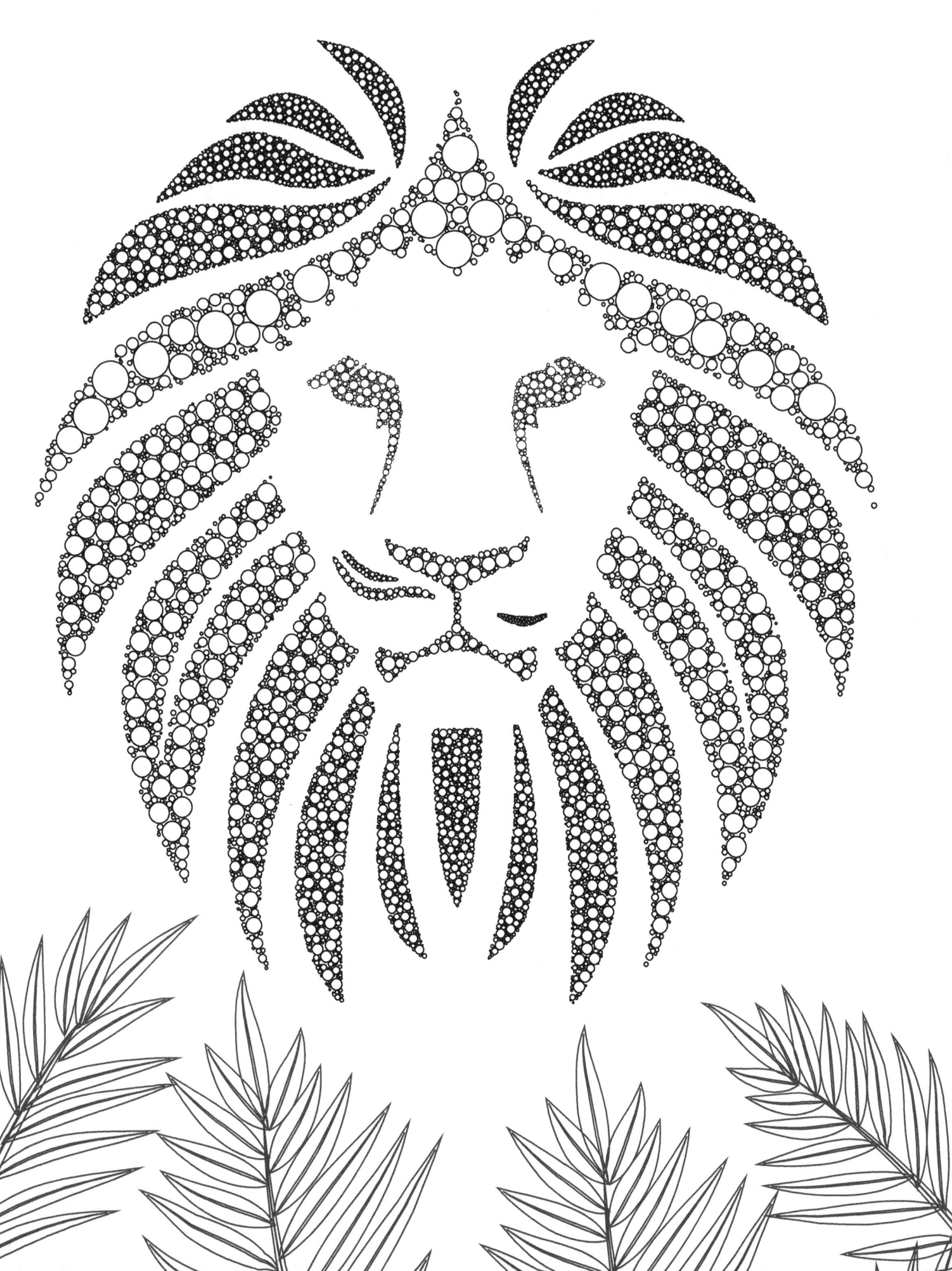

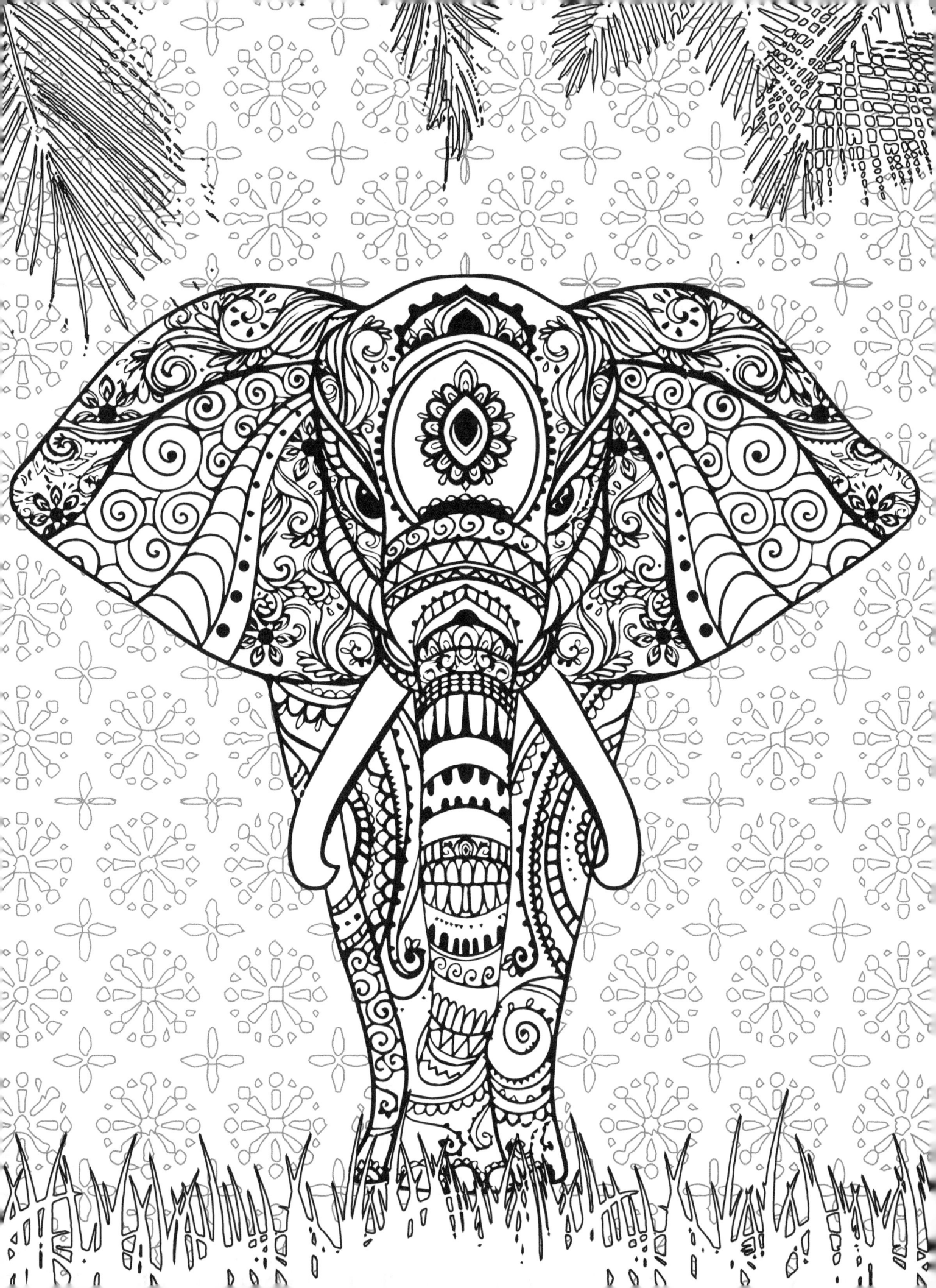

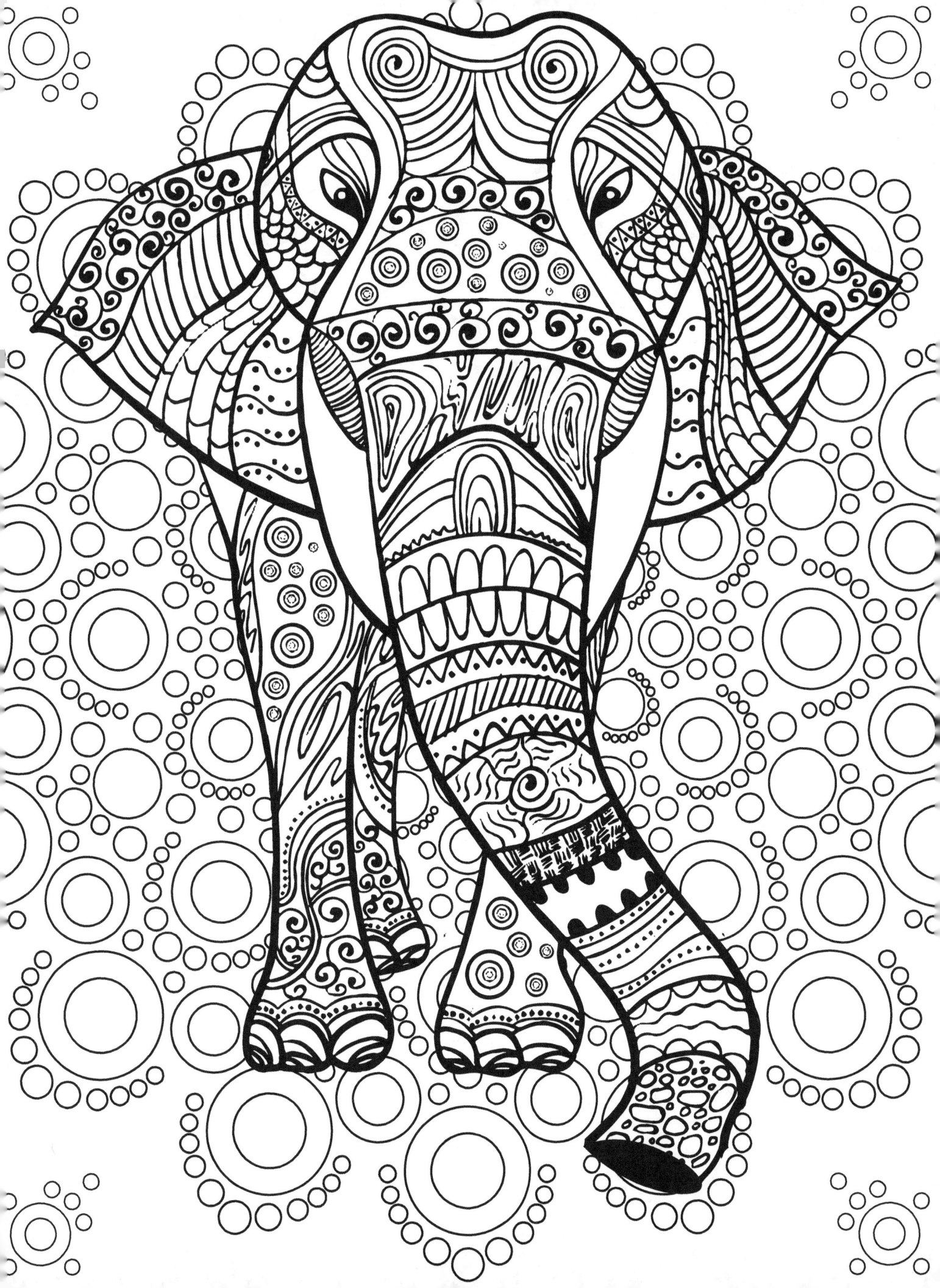

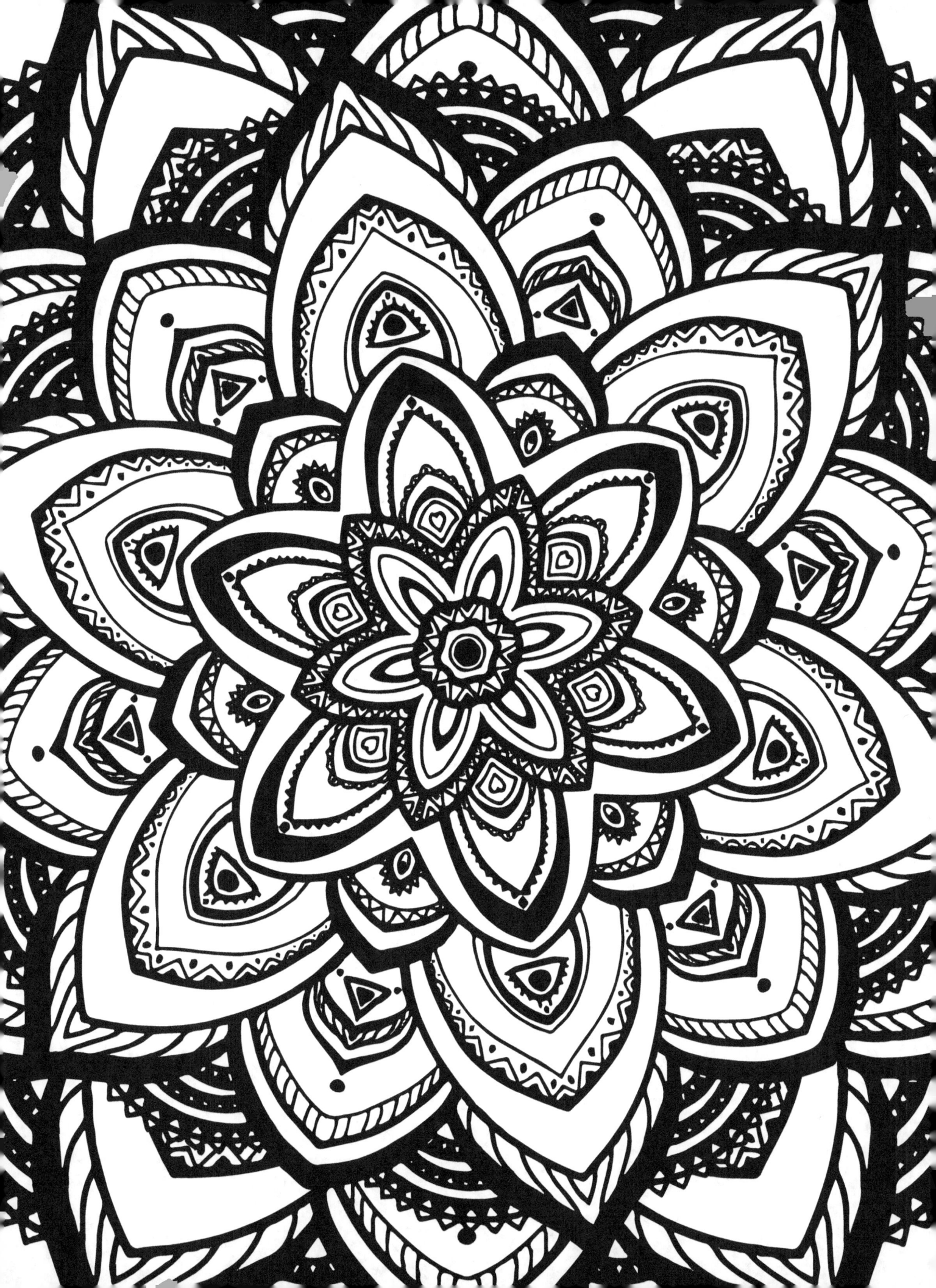

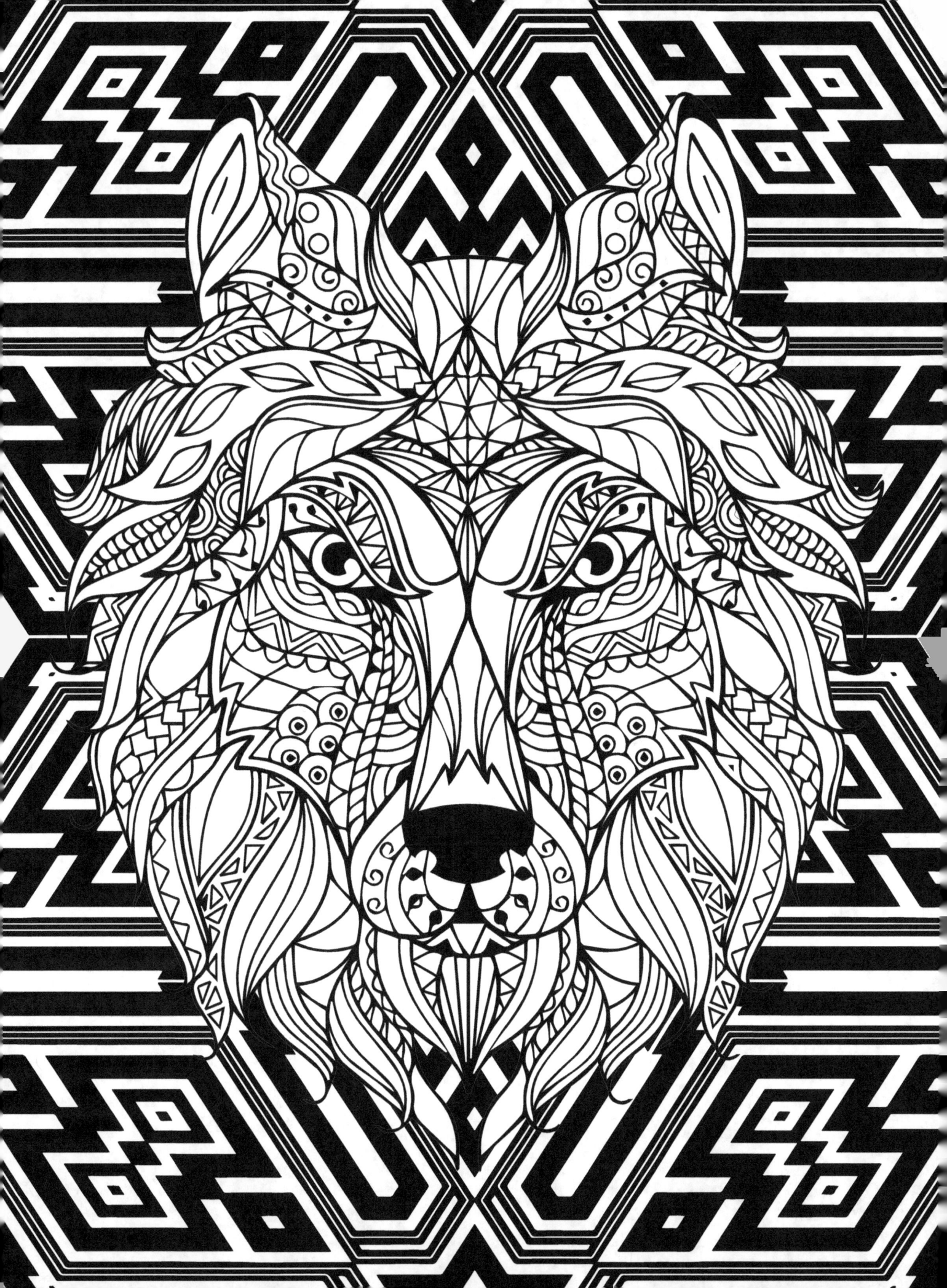

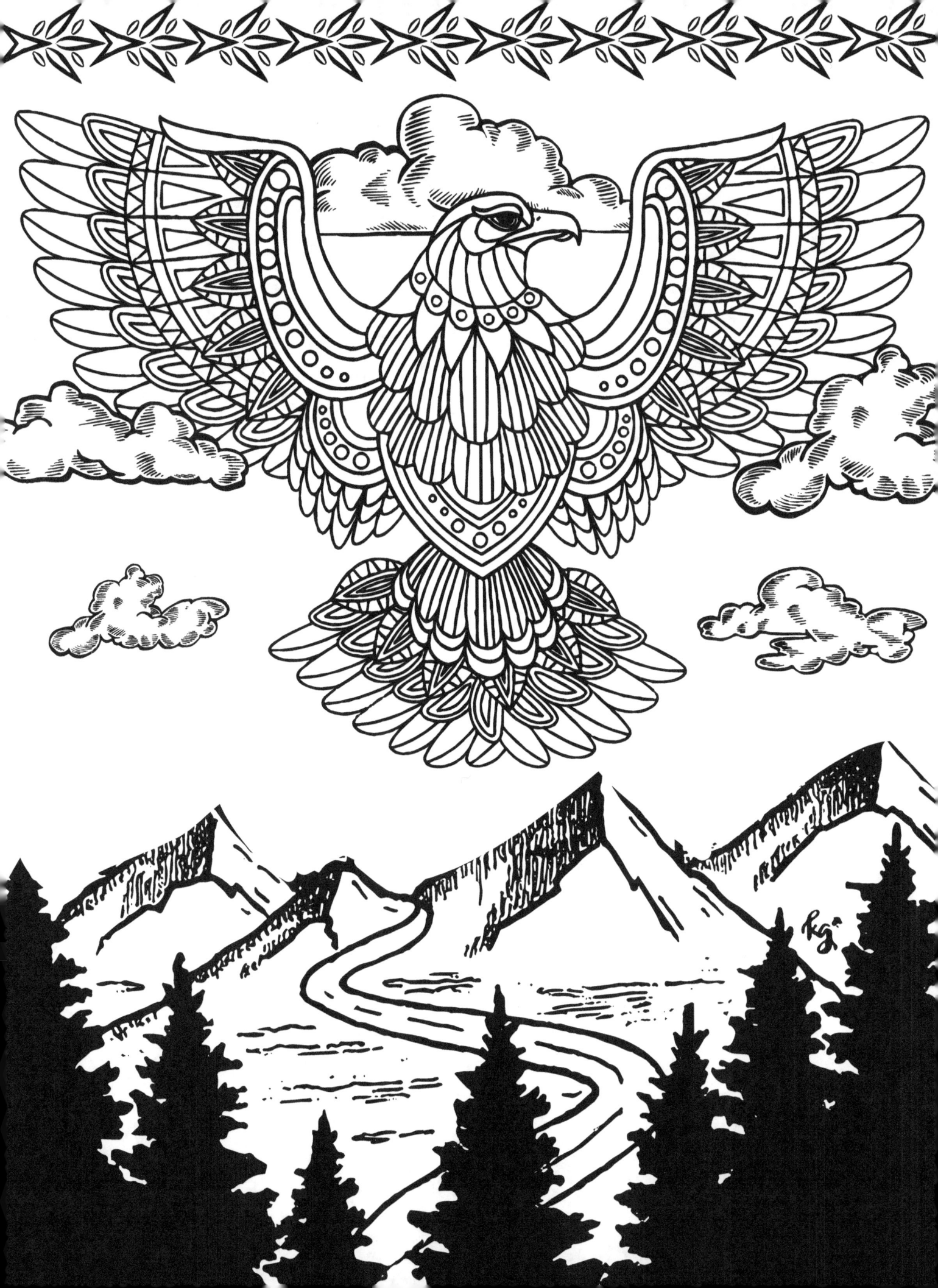

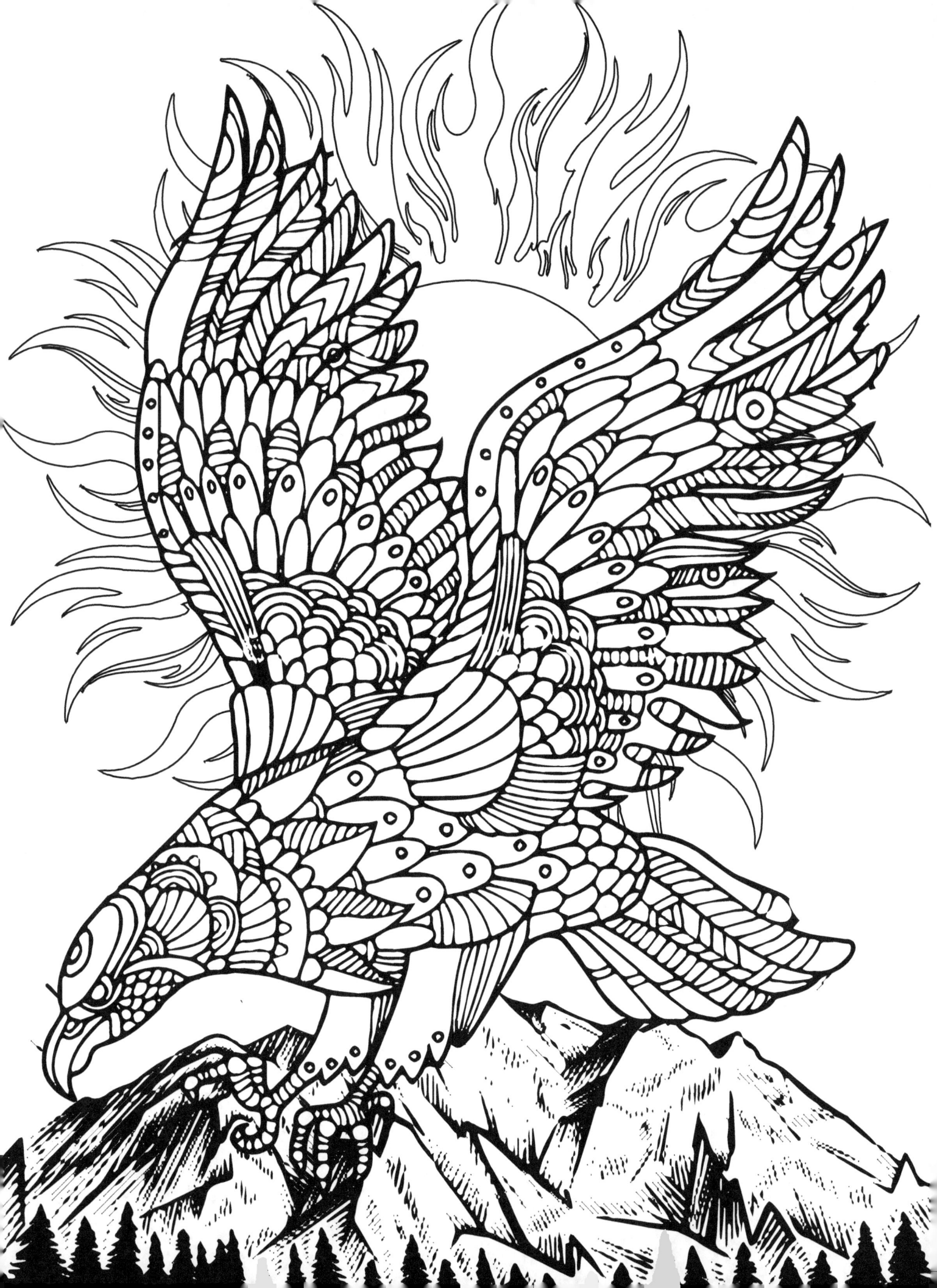

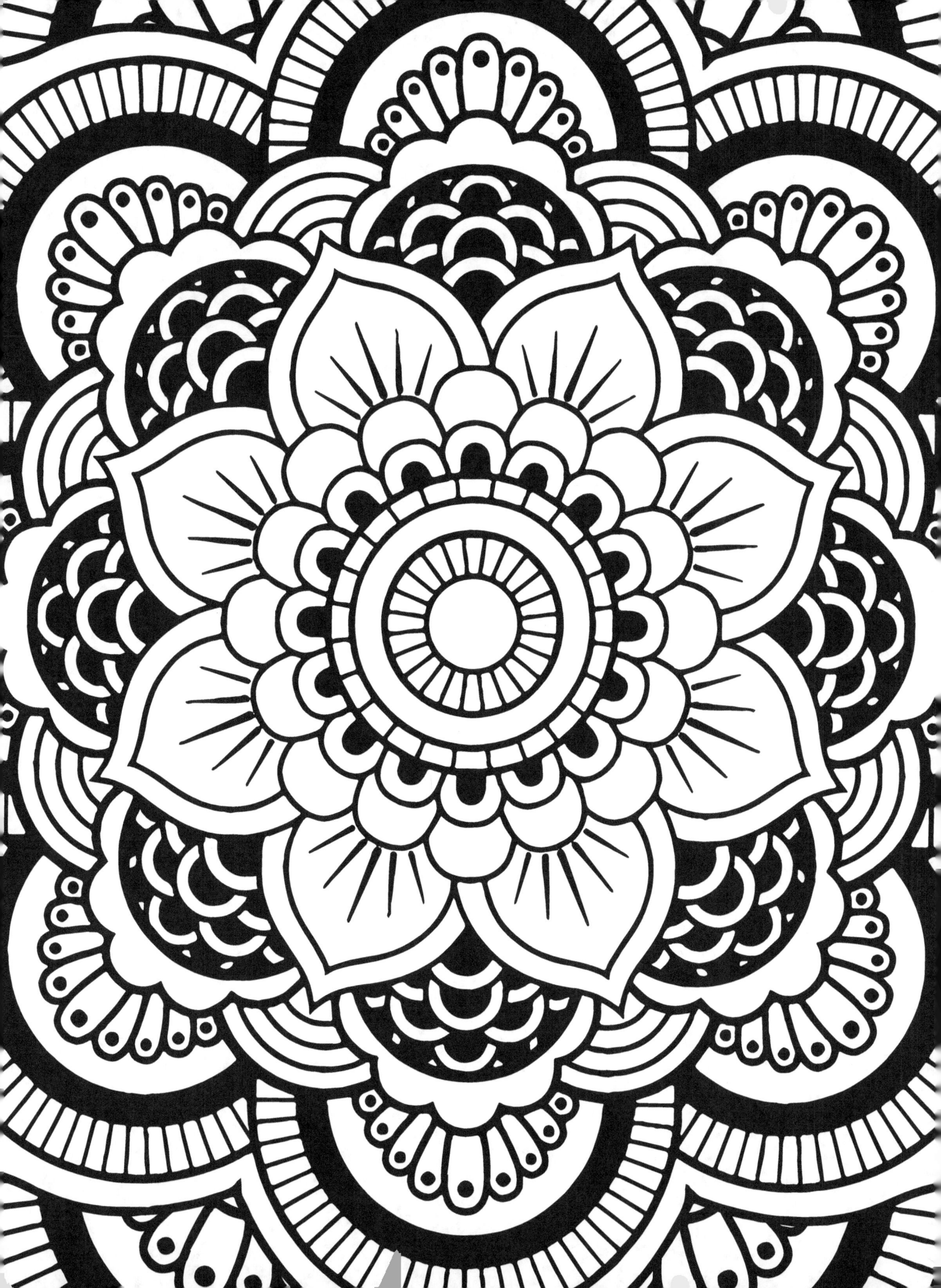

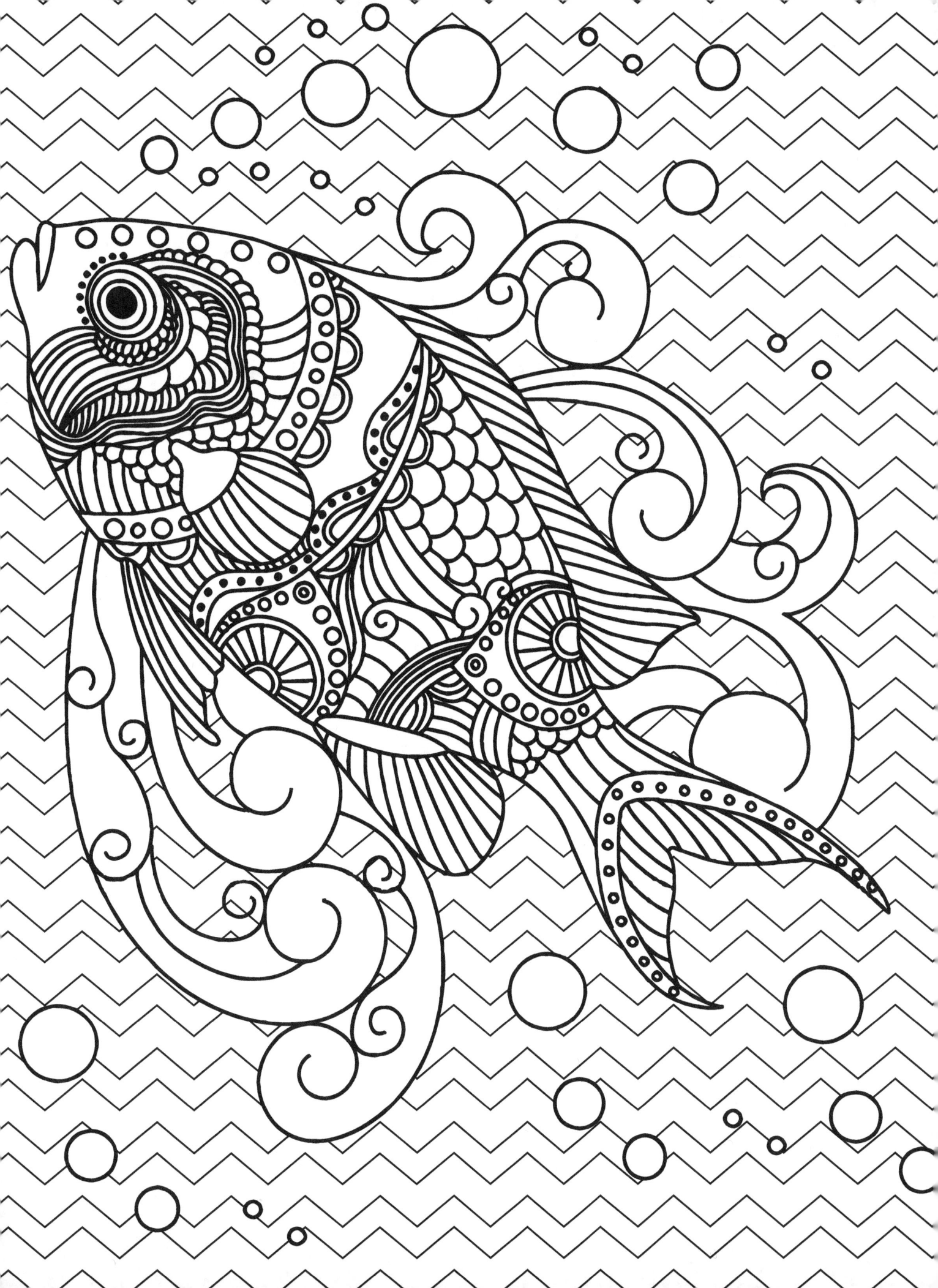

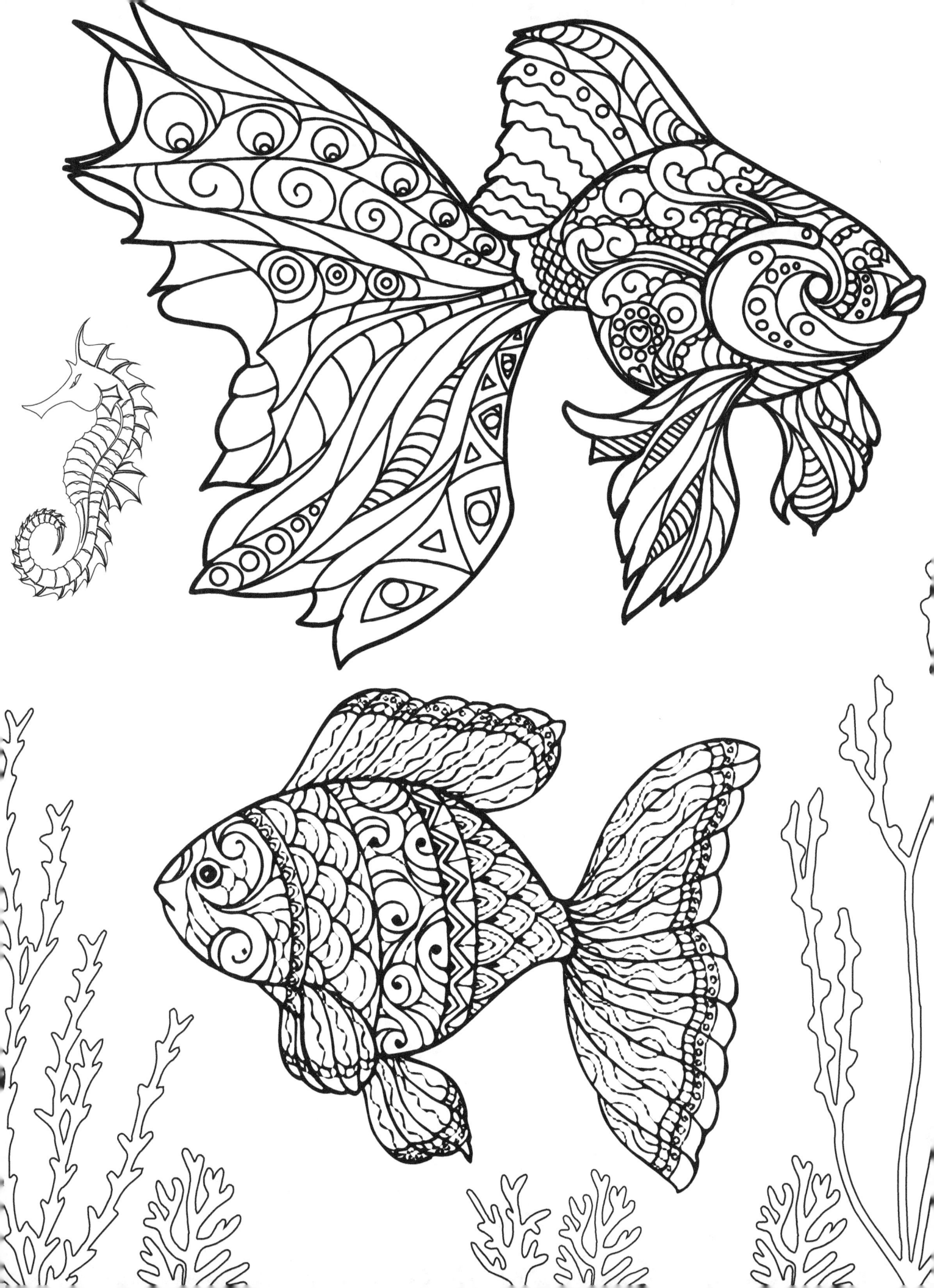

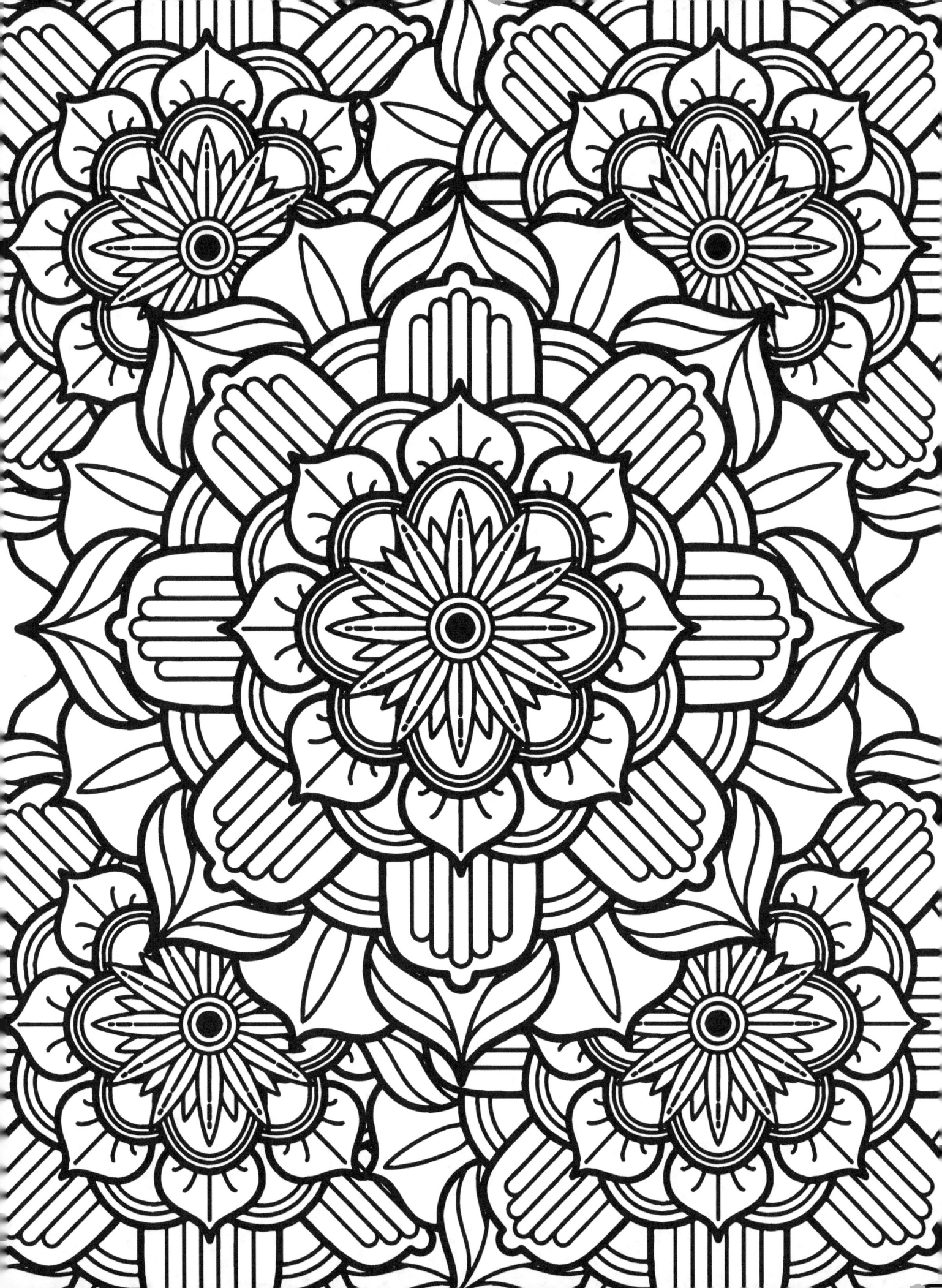

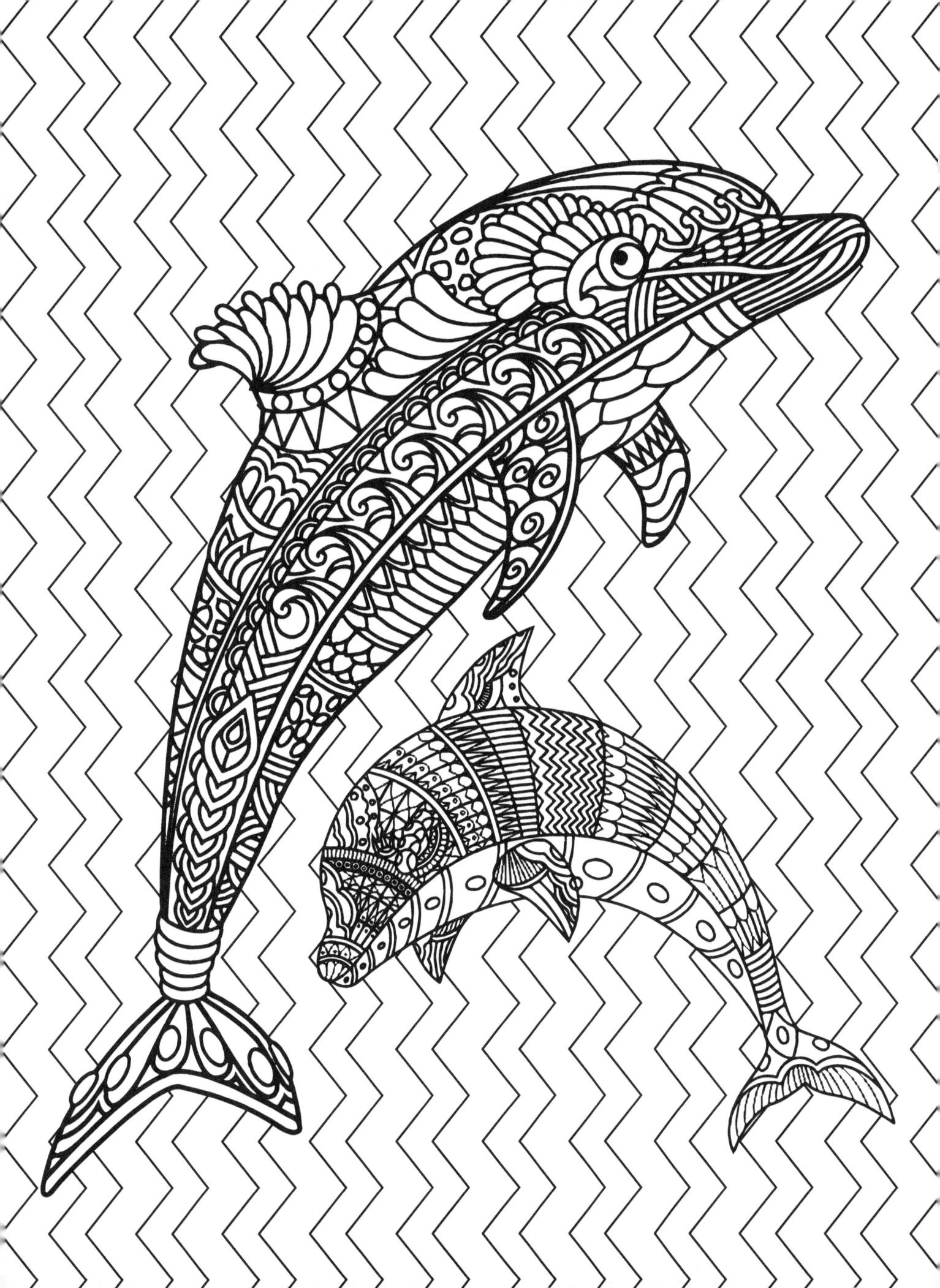

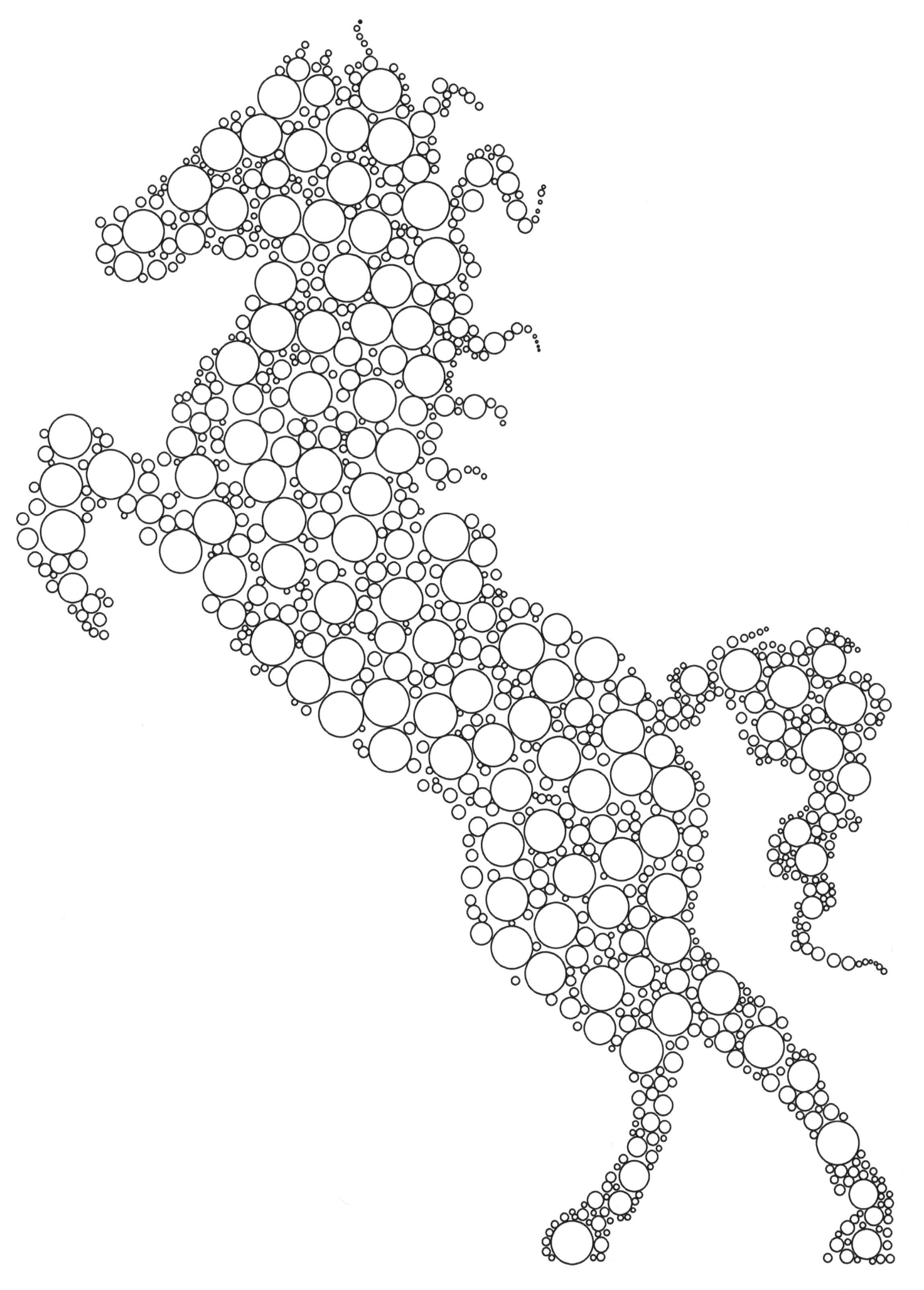

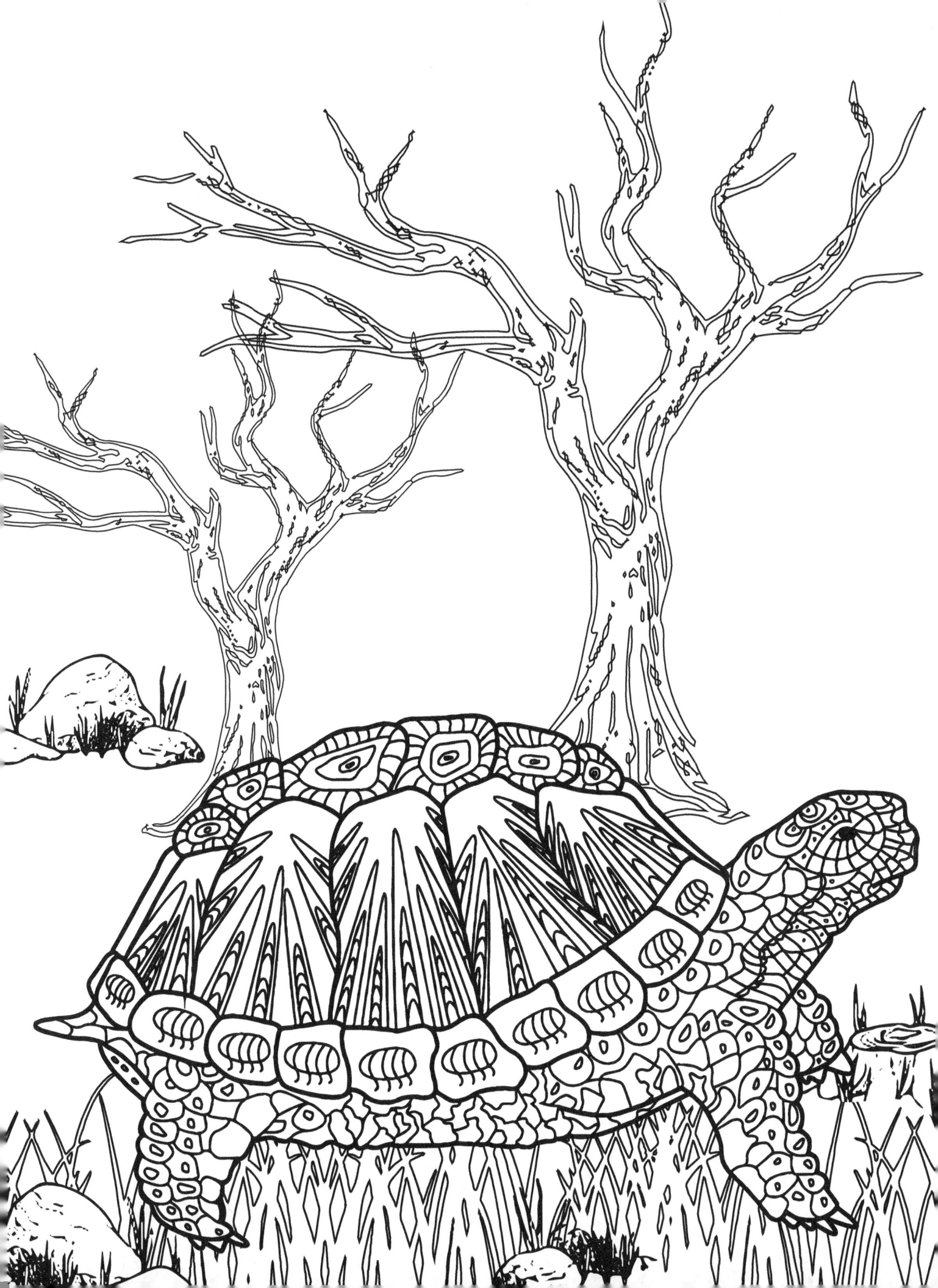

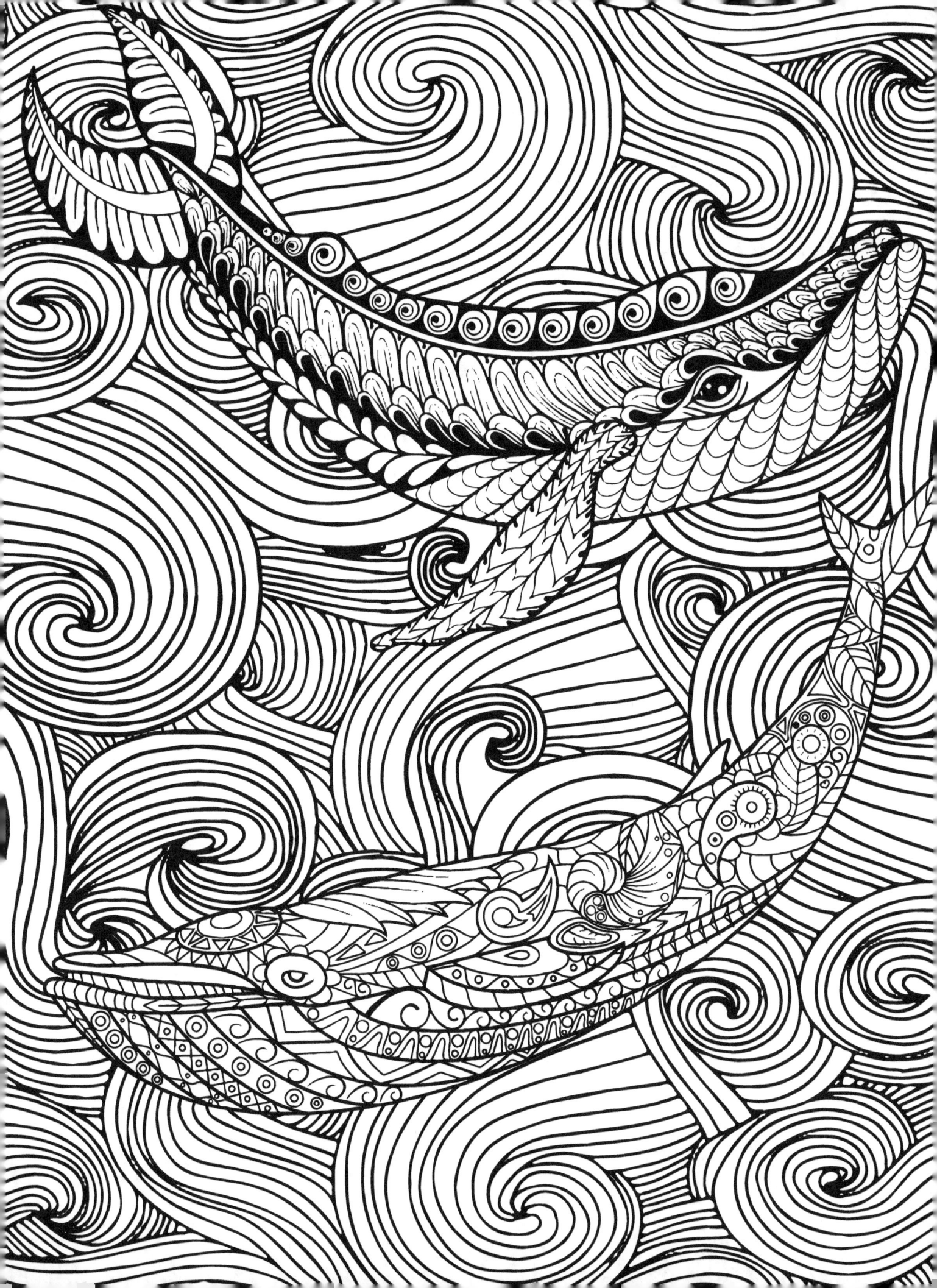

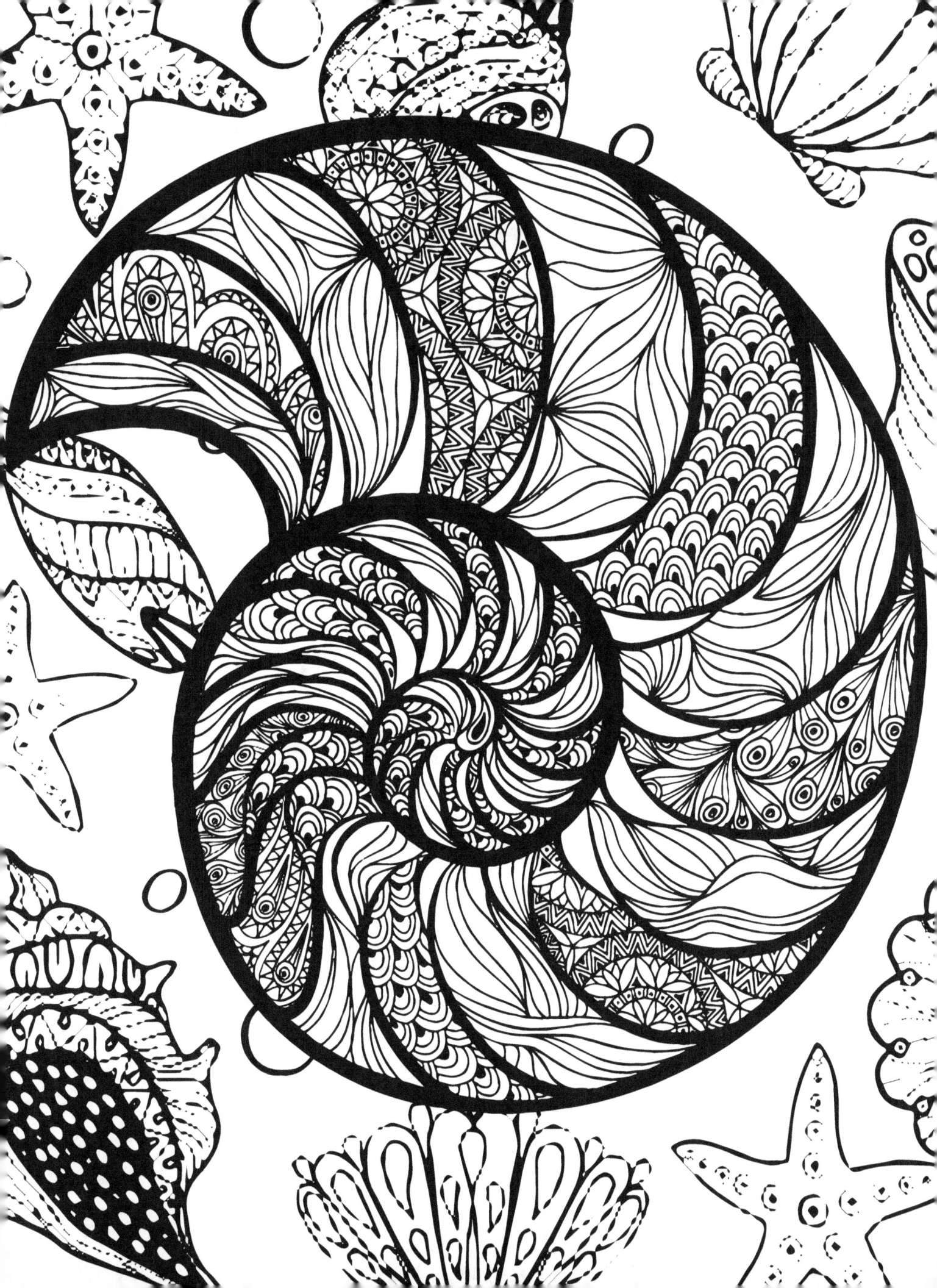

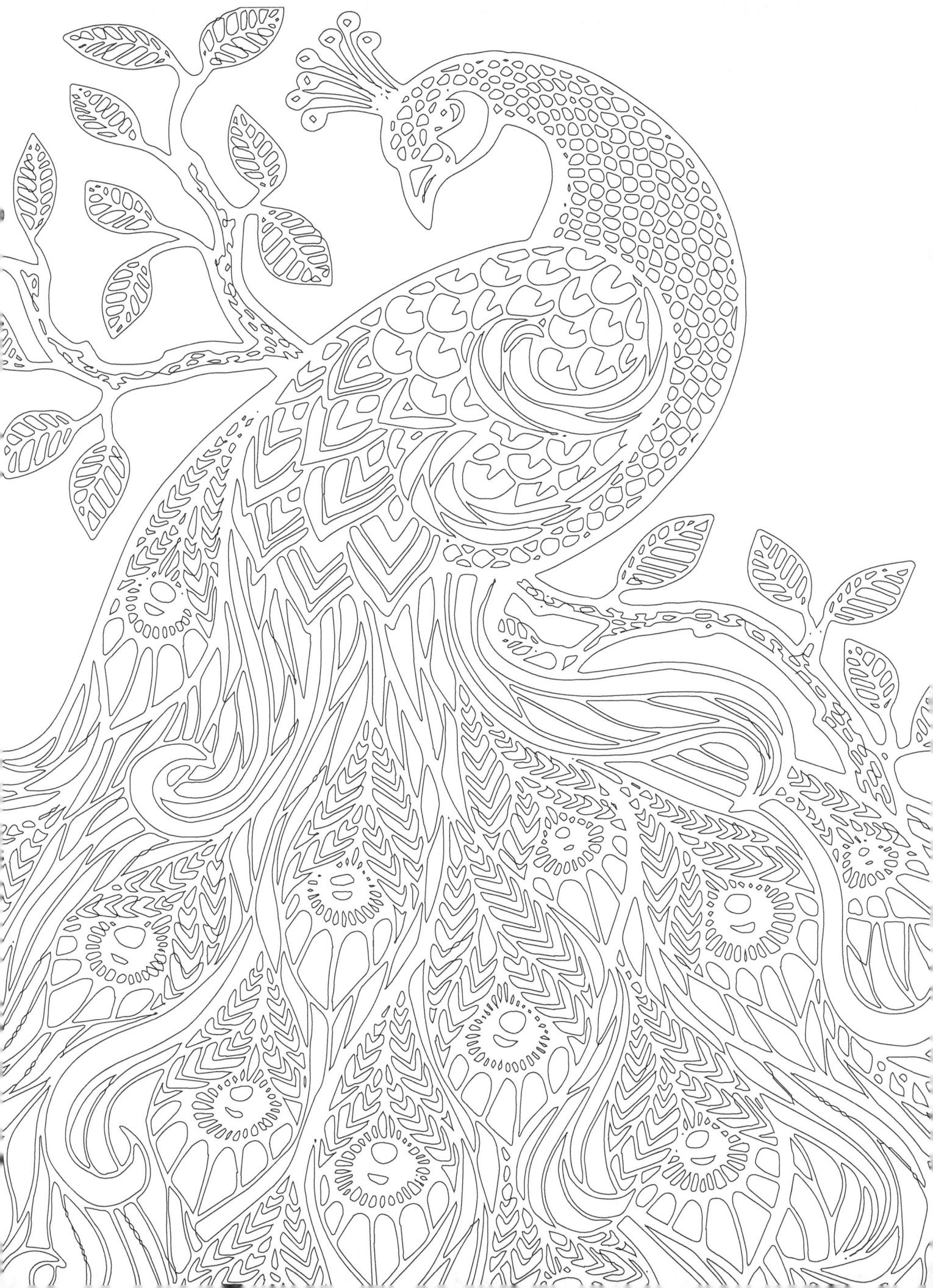

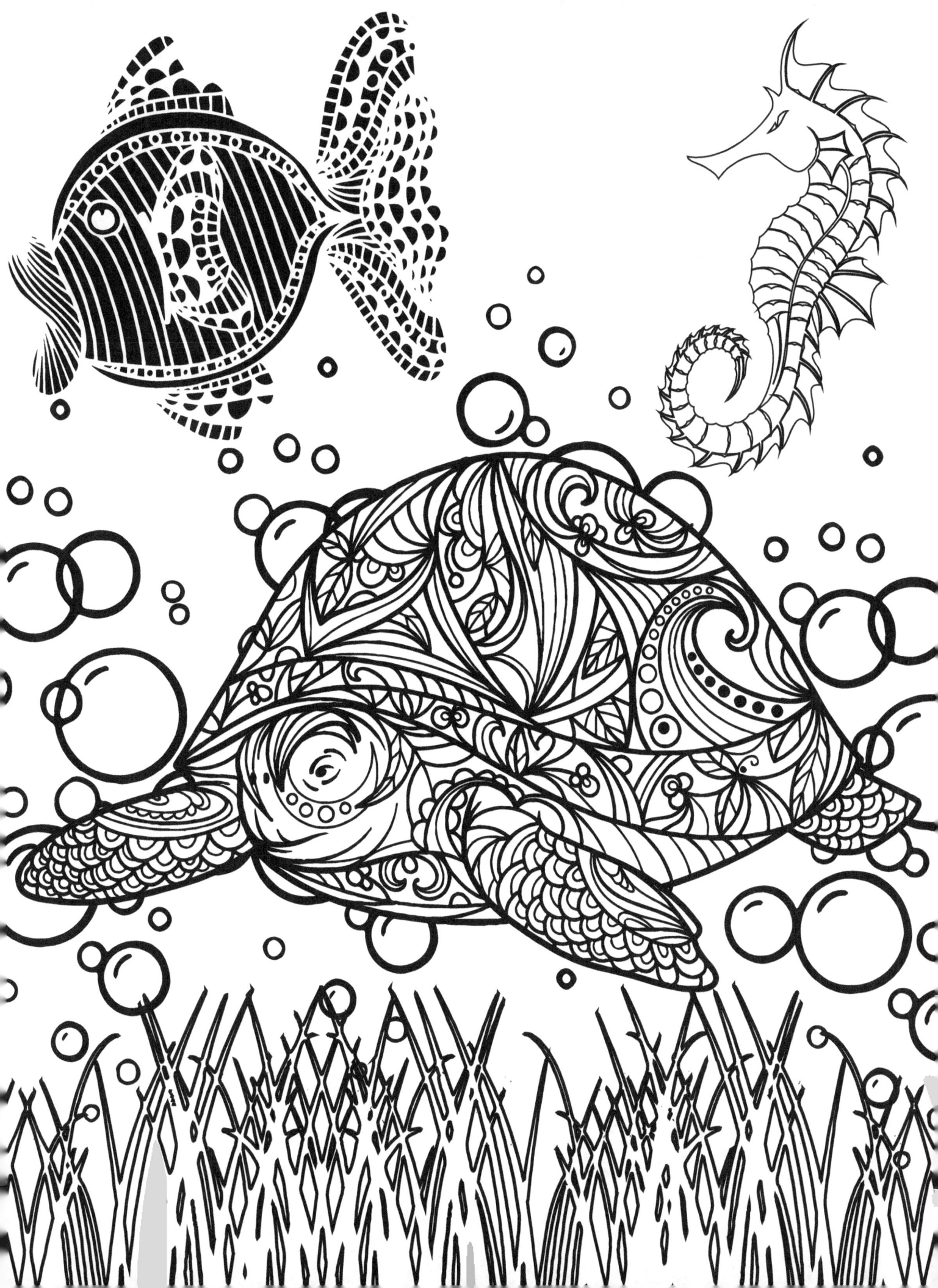

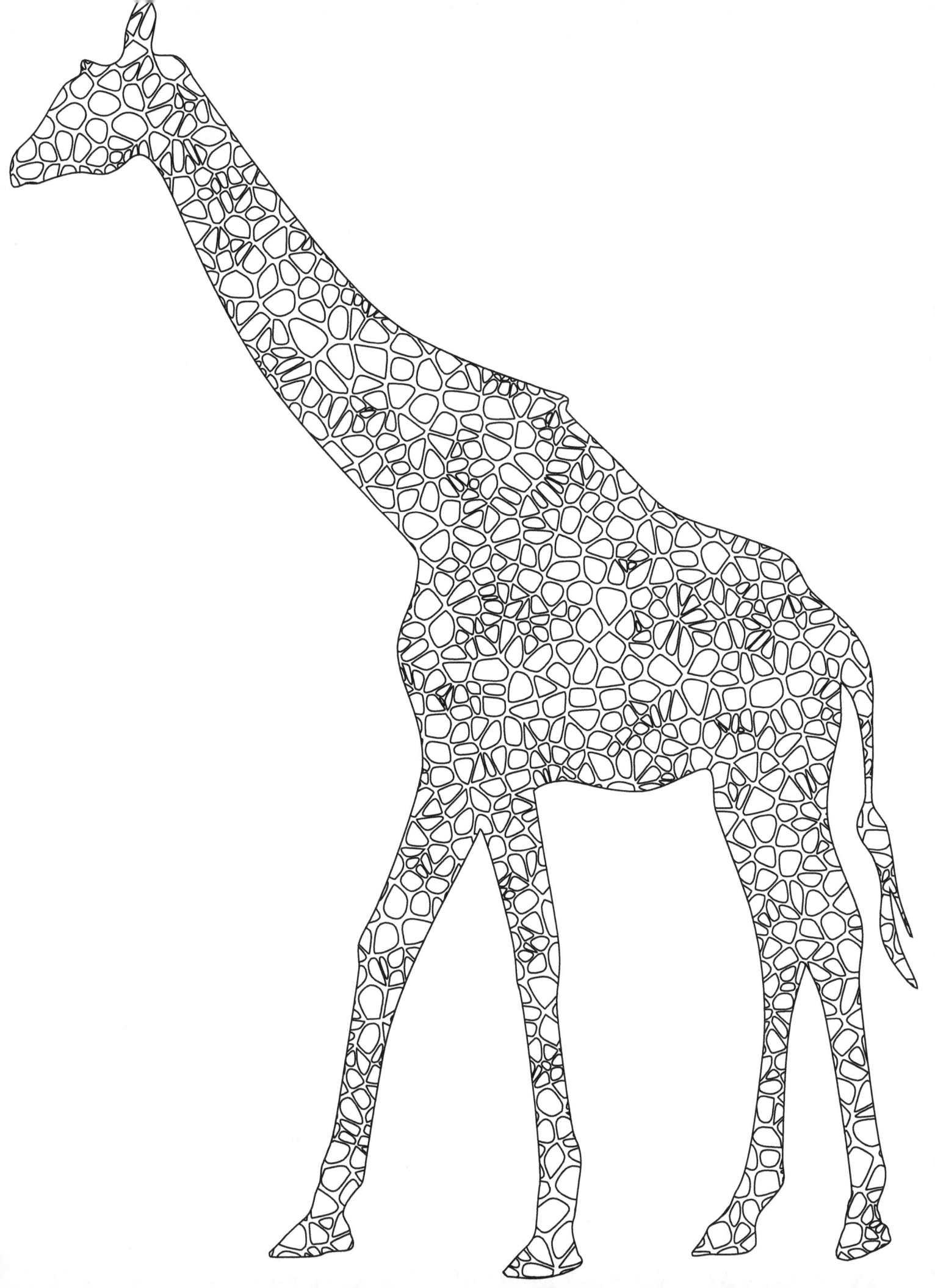

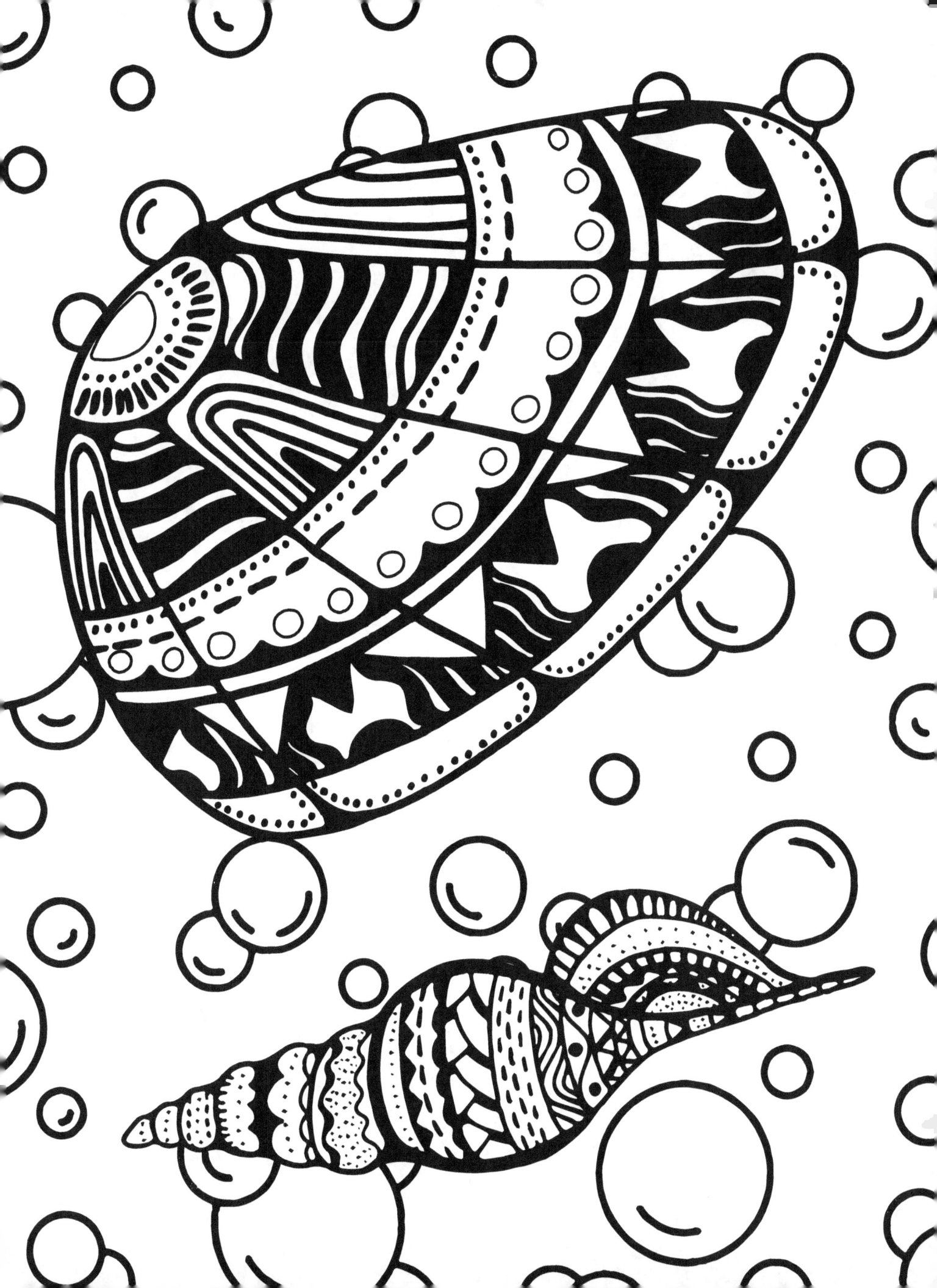

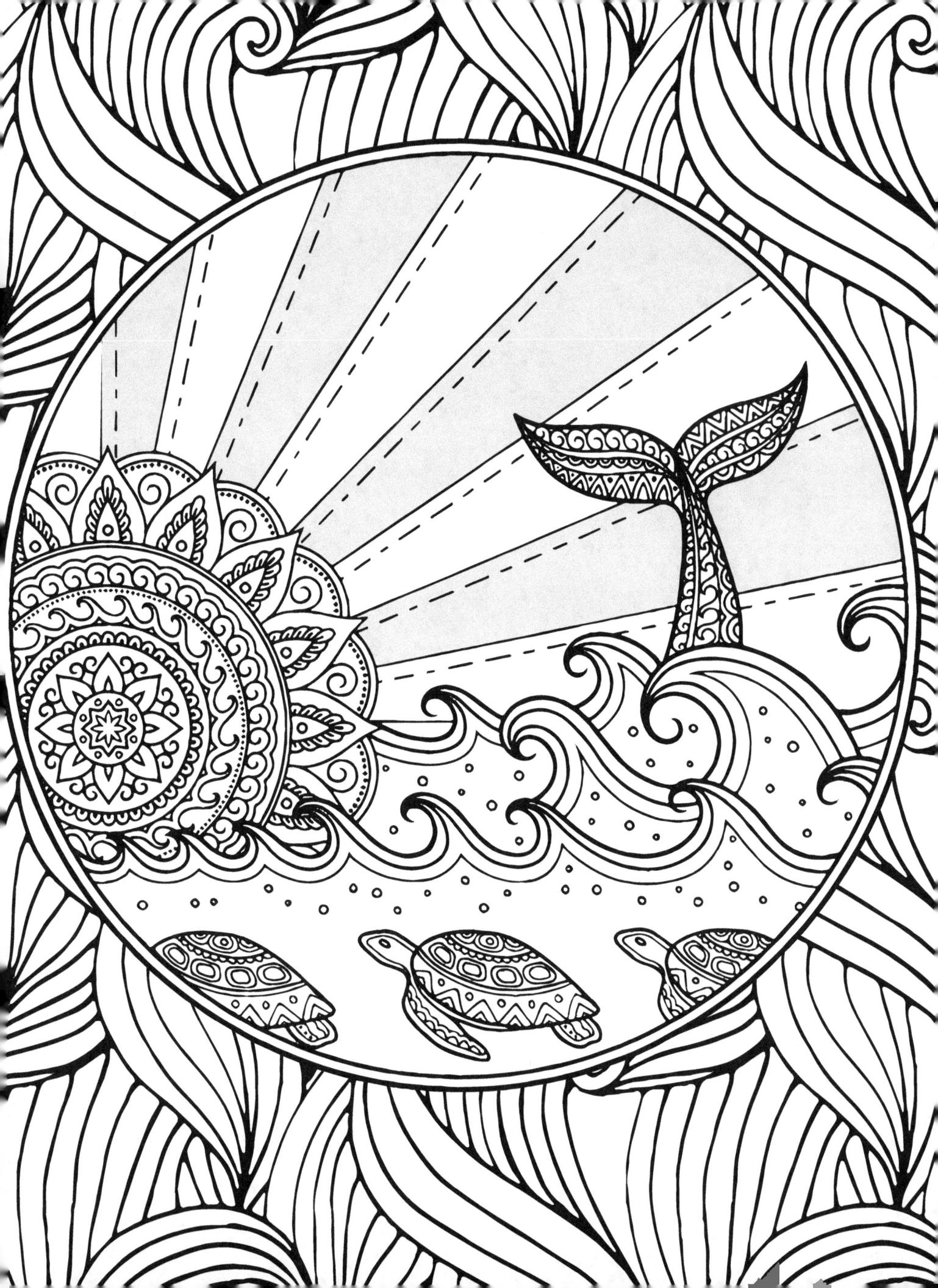

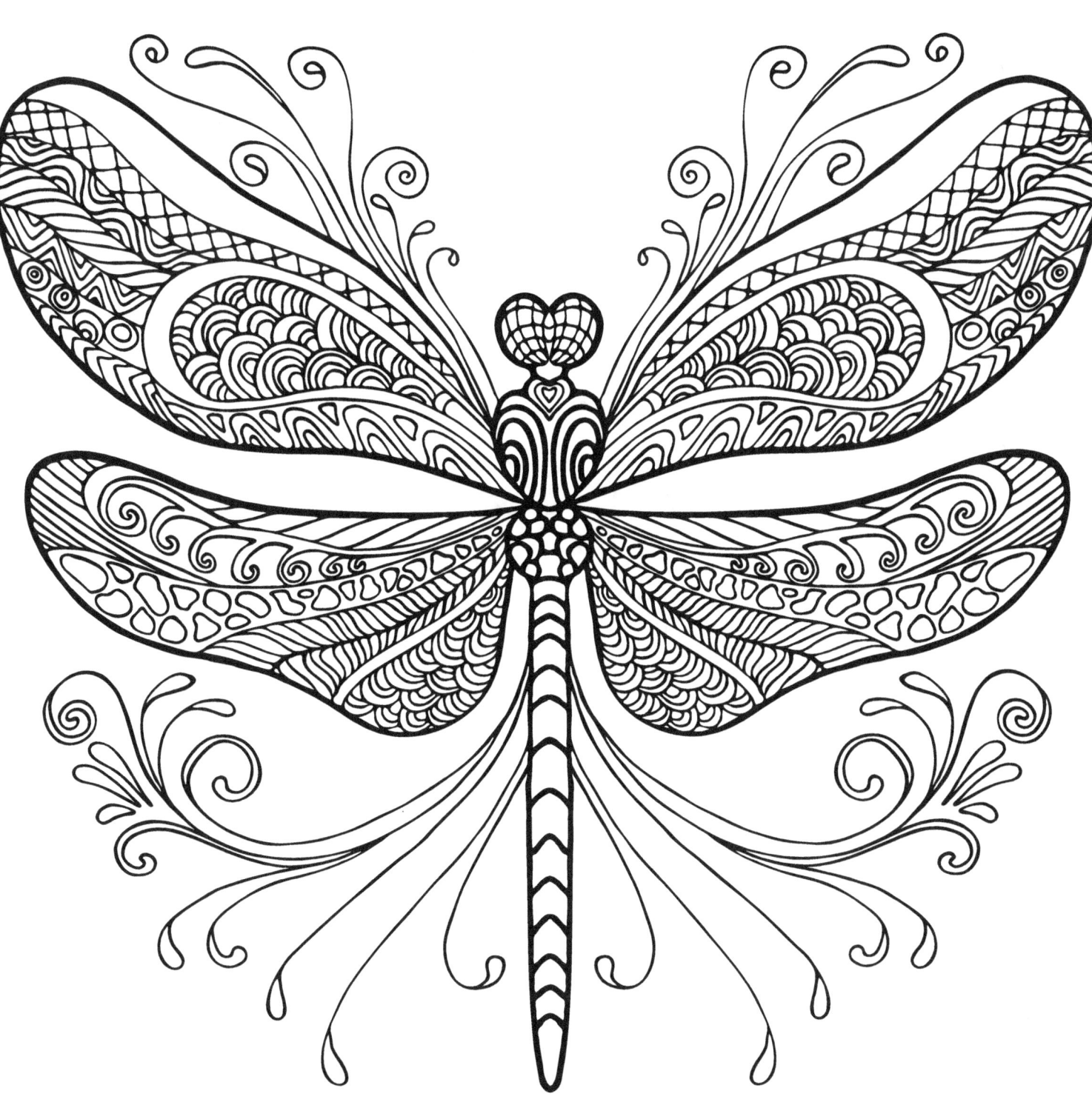

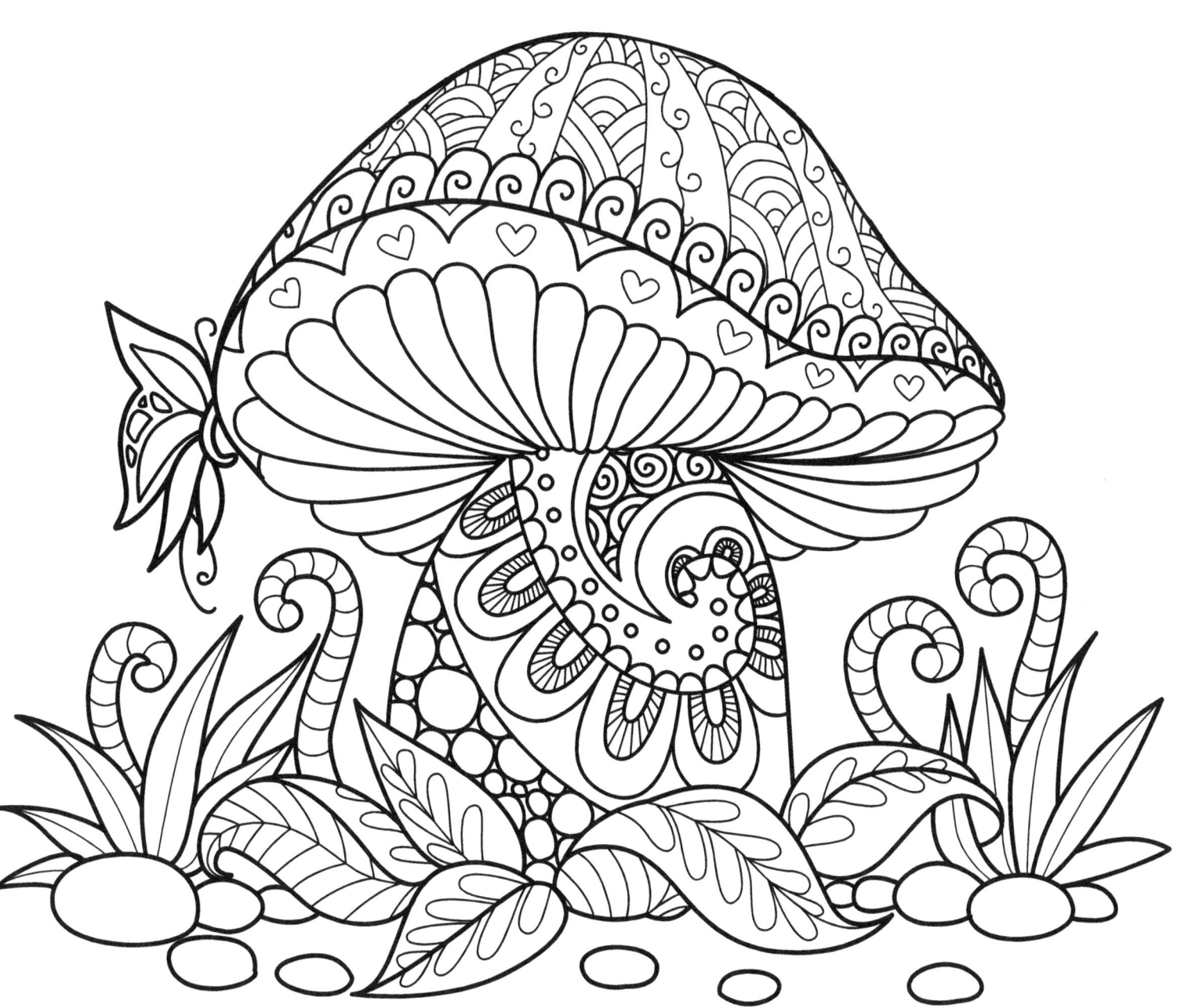